What Would You Do?

What Would You Do?

By Leland B. Jacobs

Drawings by Frank Carlings

GARRARD PUBLISHING COMPANY
CHAMPAIGN, ILLINOIS

Copyright © 1972 by Leland B. Jacobs   All rights reserved. Manufactured in the U.S.A.
International Standard Book Number: 8116–6963–7   Library of Congress Catalog Card Number: 72–1772

What Would You Do?

If you had been told
To sit in a chair,
What would you do
If you weren't sitting there?
    Think!
        What would you do?

Would you lead
A parade
Around the room?
Would you play
On a pan
With a "boom, boom, boom"?
      Or what would you do?

If you had skates
That were shiny and new,
What kinds of tricks
Would you most like to do?
　　Tell us! Do!

If you saw red apples
Up in a tree,
Would you leave them,
Or eat them,
Or bring them to me?
      Just what would you do?

If you were a mouse
Who was chased by a cat,
What would you do
At a time like that?
      Yes, what would you do?

If you were a toad,
Would you sit by the road
And count every truck
Passing by with its load?
    Would you?
        What would you do?

If you were a bear
In a cage
In the zoo,
Would you stare
At the children
Staring at you?
        Well, would you?

If you were a bird
With a nest
In a tree,
How would you hide it
So no one could see?
      What would you do?

If you were
A jumping jack,
Would you
Jump and play?
Or might you
Spring up
From your box
And jump,
Jump, jump away?
      Say!
      What would you do?

If you were a shadow
In the sunshine
Warm and bright,
What would you do
When the sun was gone
At night?
      What would you do?

If you could be
A big old clock,
Would you say "Tick"
And then say "Tock"?
Or would you make
Some other noise
To tell the time
To girls and boys?
      Tell what you would do.

If you were
A great big truck
And the traffic light
Turned blue,
Instead of being
Red or green,
Just what
Would you do?
      Yes, what would you do?

If you were a spider,
Would you sit in the sun
When you'd spun and you'd spun,
And your spinning was done?
If you were a spider,
Would you sit in the shade
When you'd spun and you'd spun,
And your web had been made?
    What would you do?

If in a circus
You were a horse,
You'd have to do
A stunt, of course.
    Would you prance?
    Would you dance?
        Or what would you do?

If you were a cow,
Would you eat hay,
Or to the farmer
Might you say,
"I want ice cream
To eat today"?
    What might you do?

What would you do
If you were a goat?
Would you
Put on a coat
For a ride
In a boat?
      What would you do?

If you were a clown,
Would you smile?
Would you frown?
Would you ride
On a mule?
Would you slip
And fall down?
      Just what would you do?

If you were the king
And you went to town,
Would you let the children
Try on your crown?
        Well, would you?

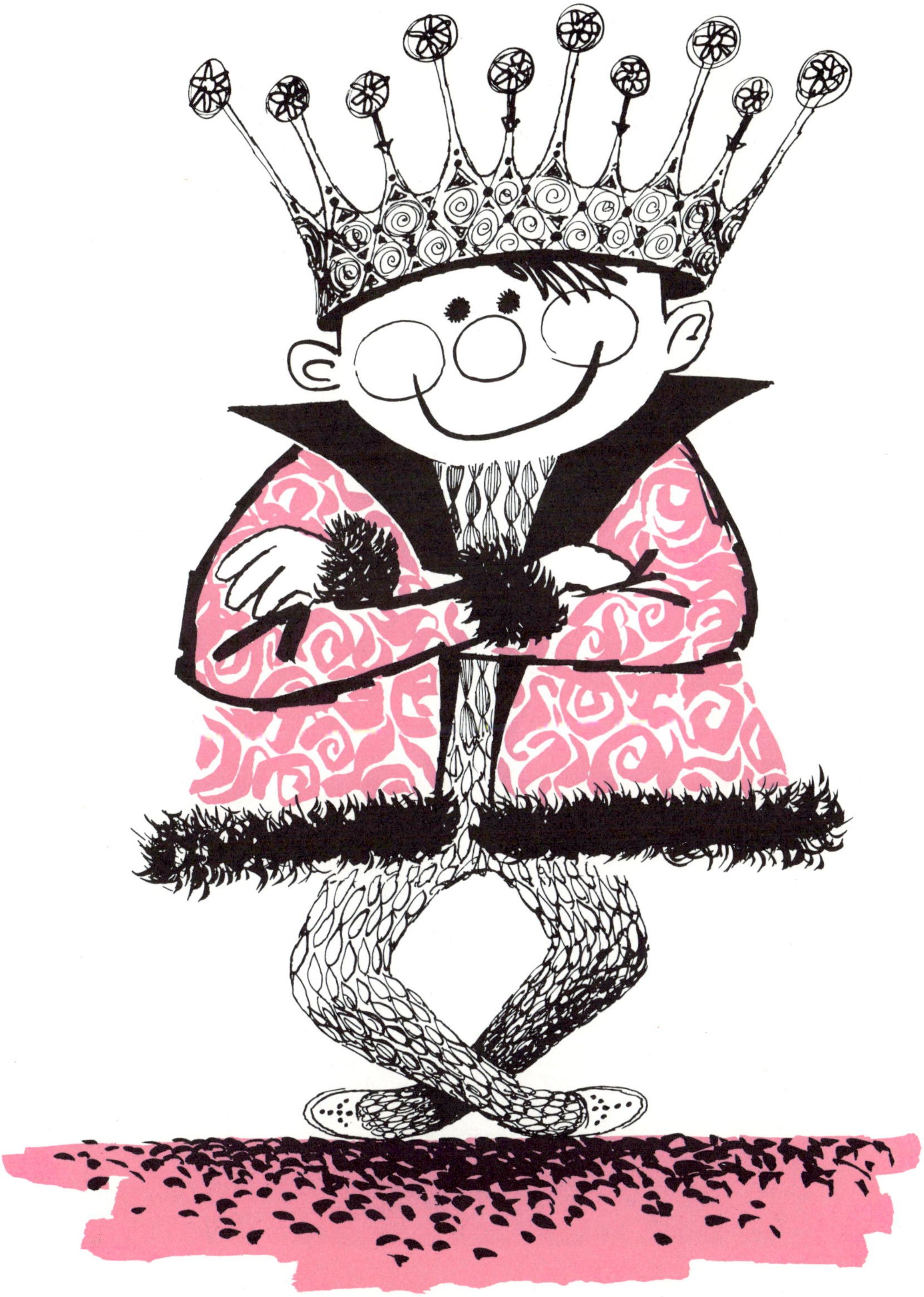

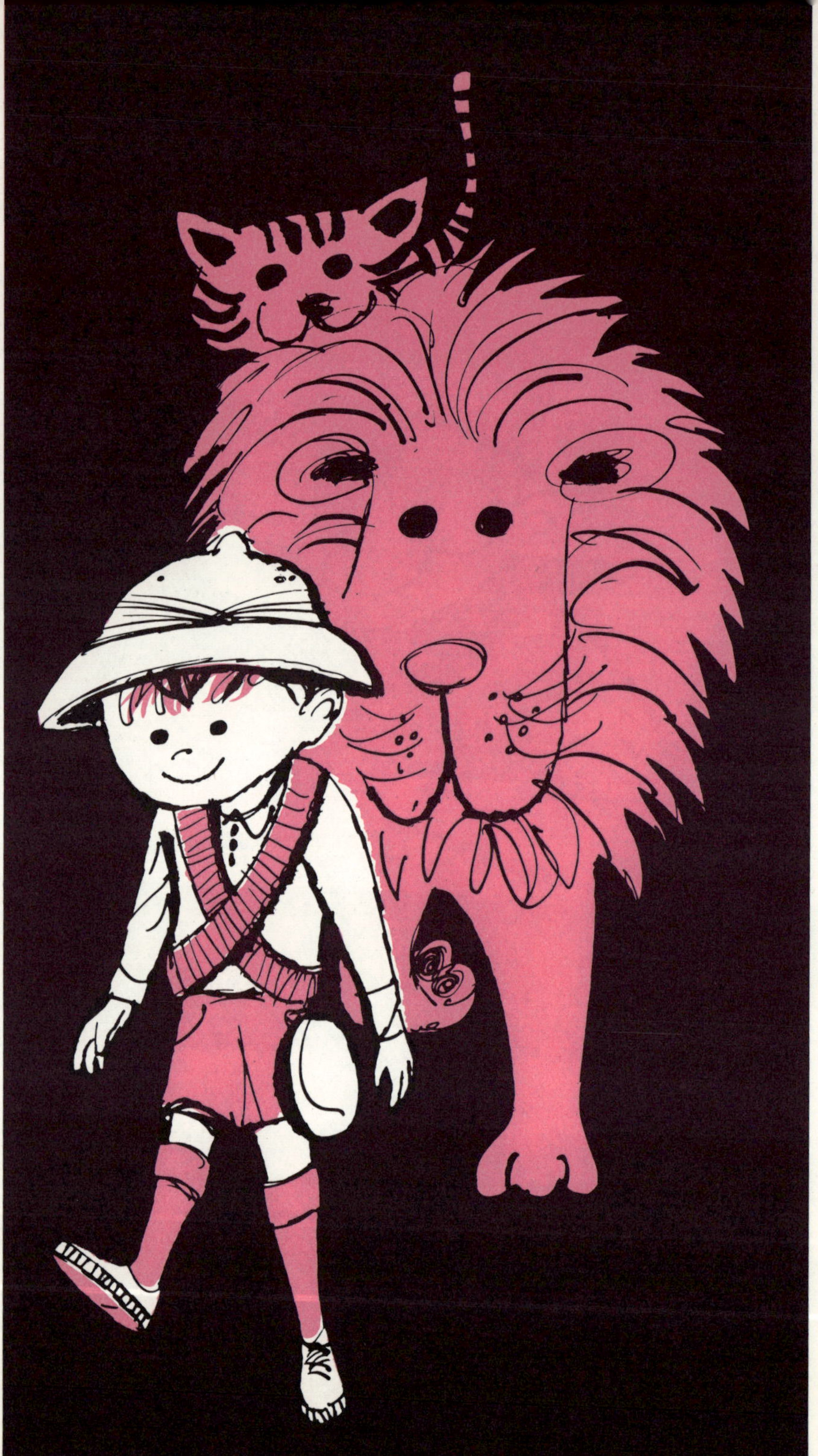

If a lion and a tiger
Were following you,
Would you lead them
Into the nearest zoo?
Or take them home?
      Or what would you do?

If you were a teacher—
A teacher, I say—
Would you be happy
To see children play,
And would you make plans
For some playtime each day?
        Would you do that?

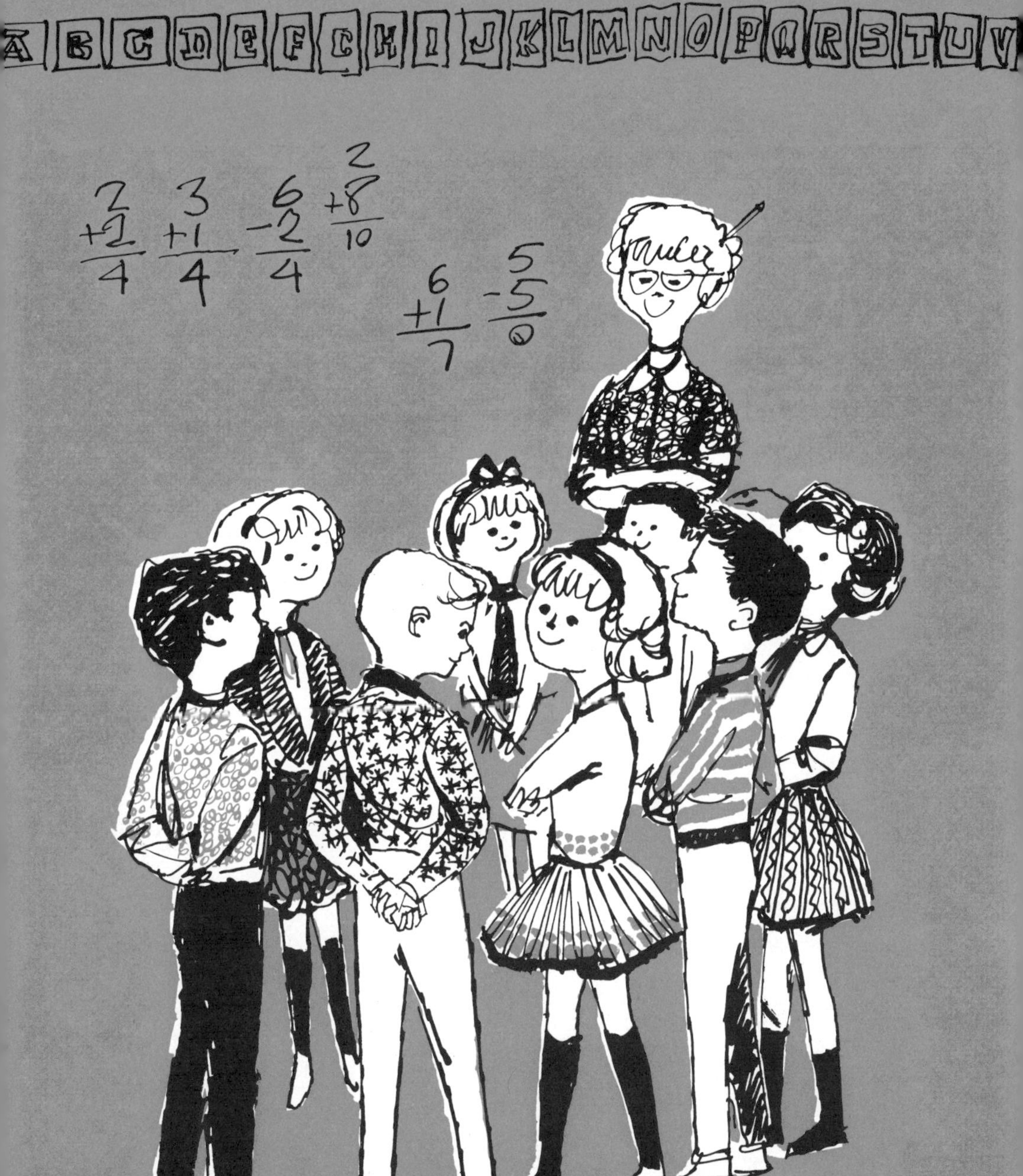
A B C D E F G H I J K L M N O P Q R S T U V
2 +2 4
3 +1 4
6 −2 4
2 +8 10
6 +1 7
5 −5 0

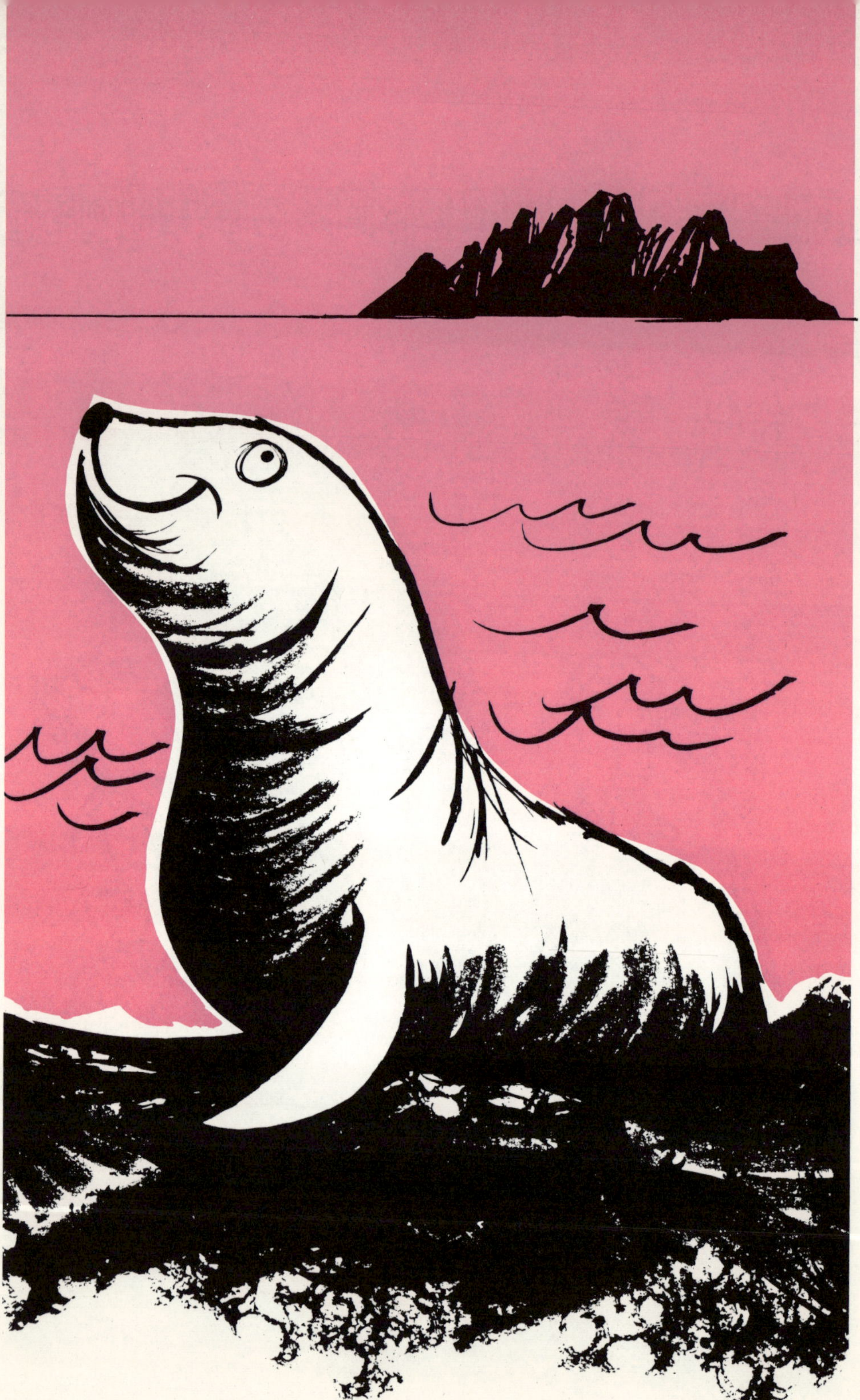

If you were a seal
In the sea
Blue and deep,
What would you do
For a place
You could sleep?
    Oh, what would you do?

If you were a kitten,
And you heard
Your mother mew,
But it was
Your bedtime,
What would you do?
          Yes, what would you do?

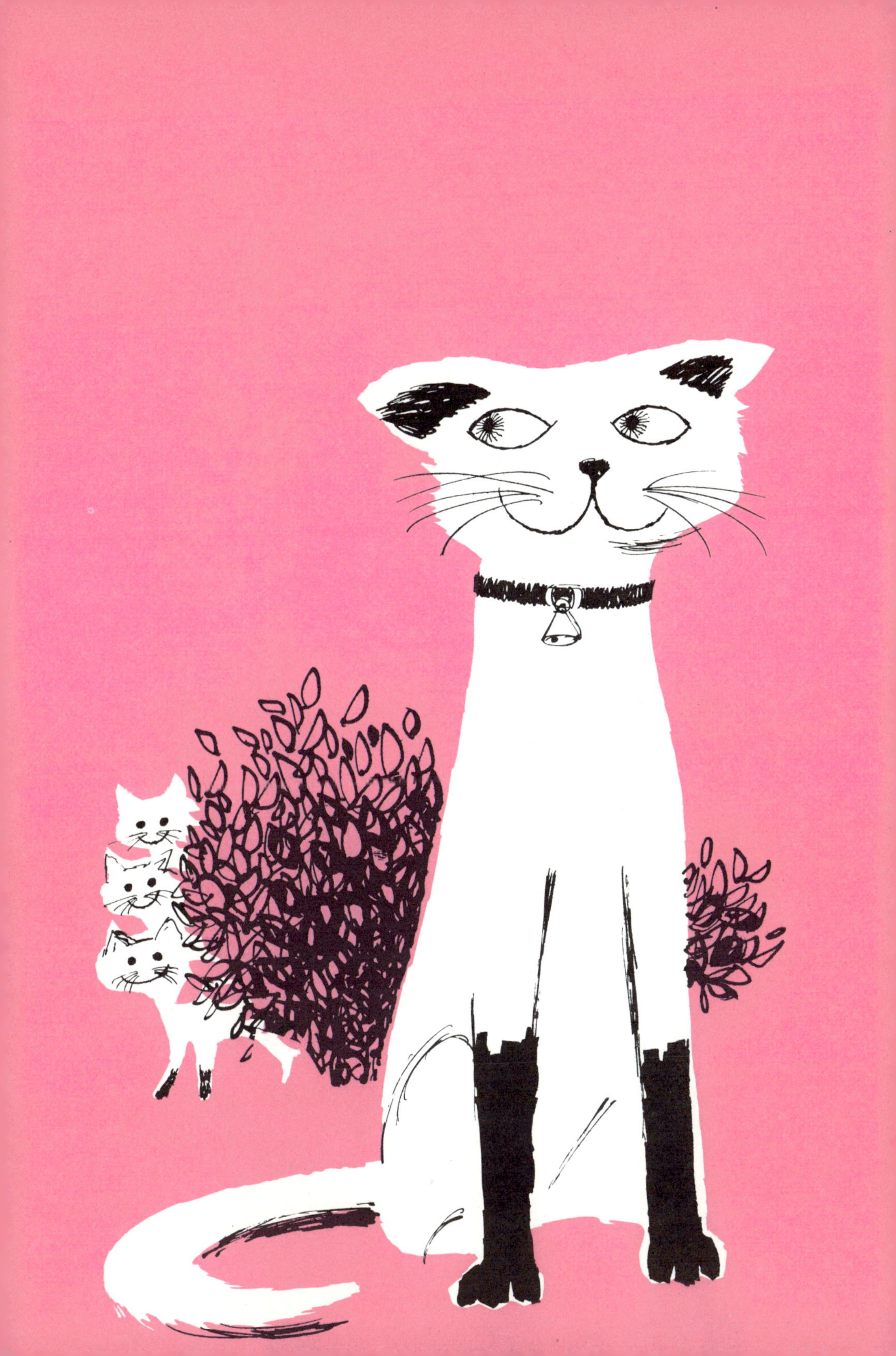

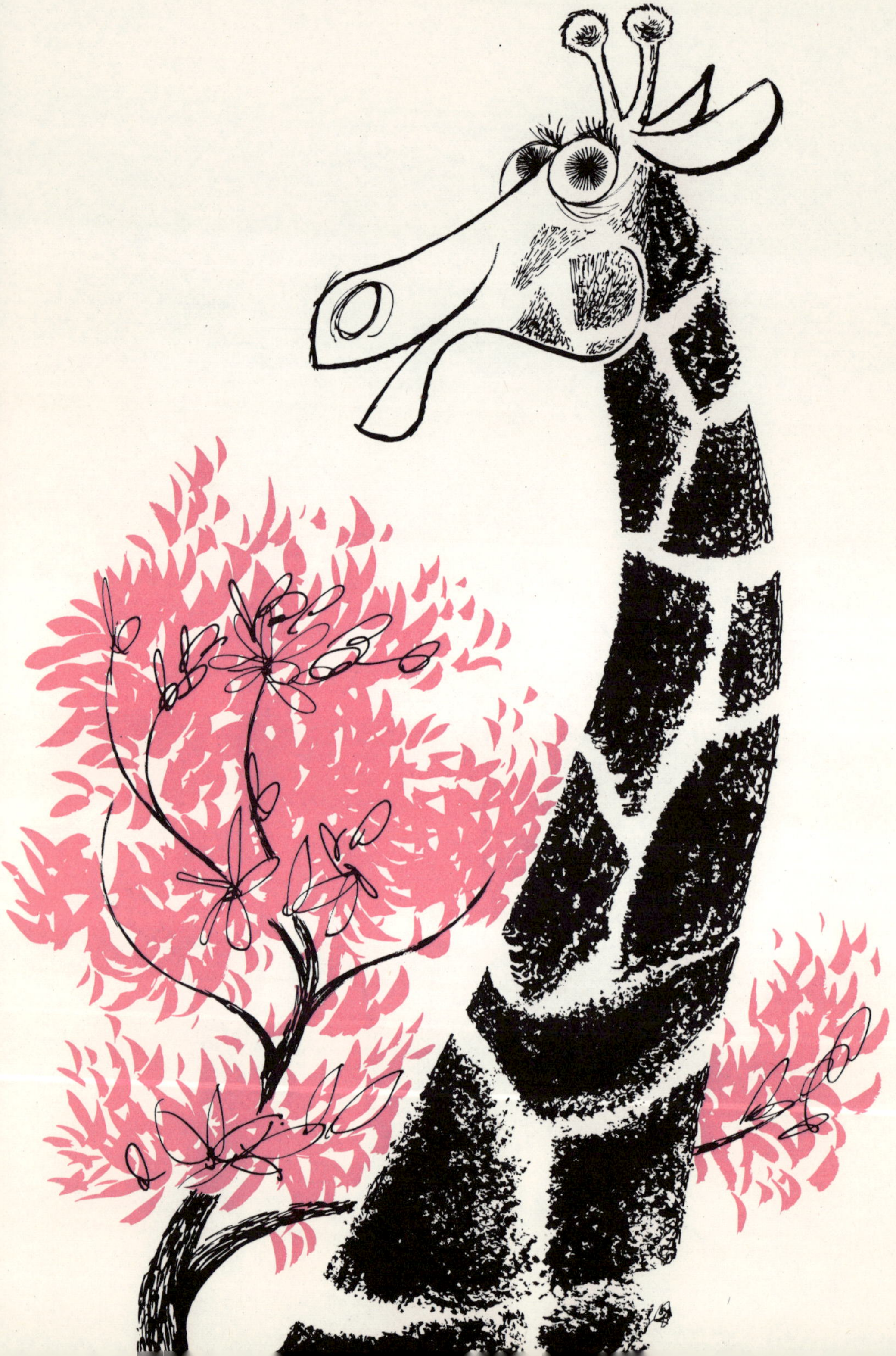

If you had a neck
Much like a giraffe,
What would you do?
Might you cry?
Might you laugh?
Might you wish
That by magic
It would shrink
About half?
        What would you do?

If you were an ostrich
And the day was very hot,
Would you strut?
Would you run?
Would you prance around a lot?
    Just what would you do?

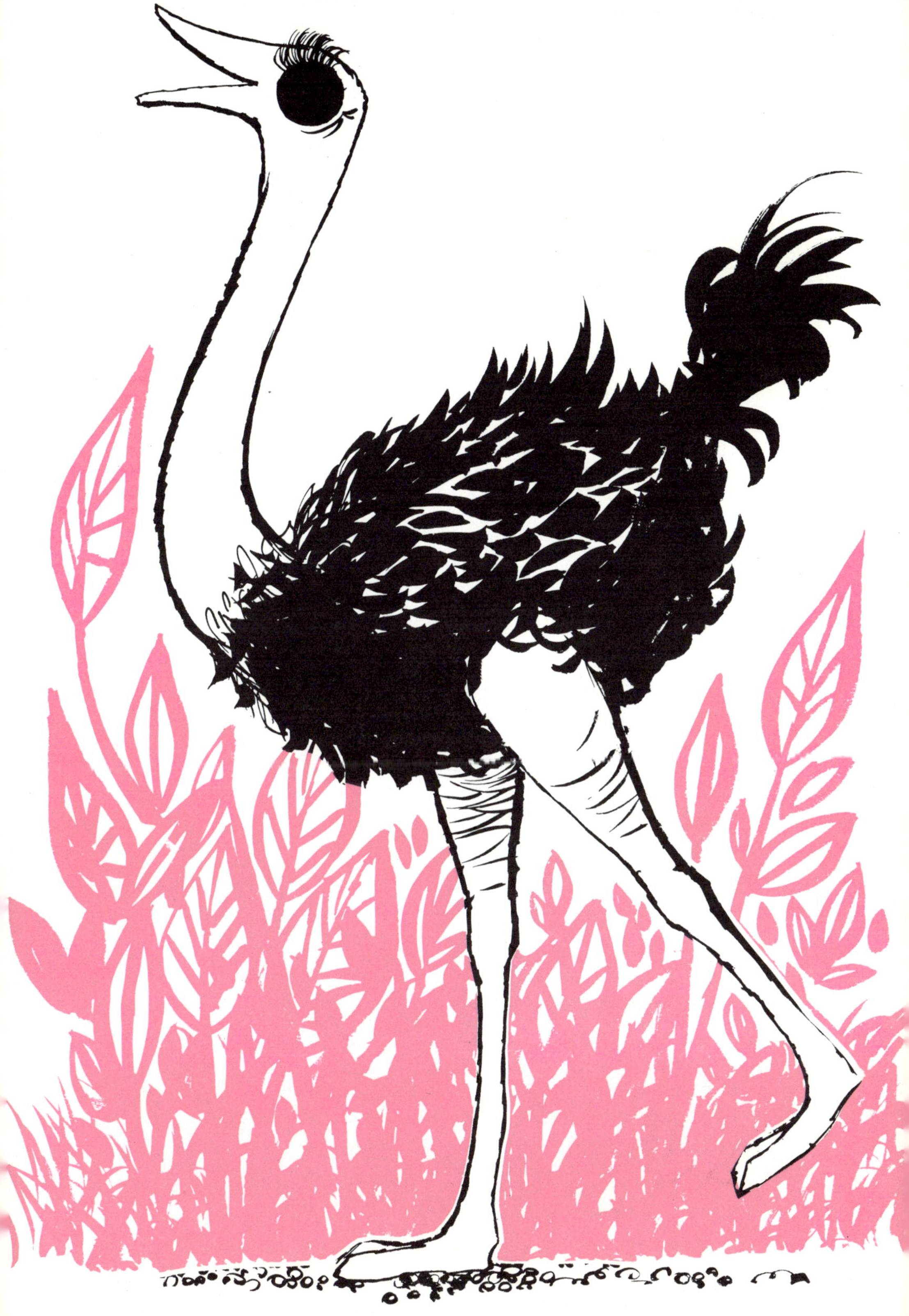

What would you do
If you were a mule?
To learn how
To "hee-haw,"
Would you go to school?
        What would you do?

If you lived in a castle
And you were a ghost,
Would you haunt on the stairway?
Would you haunt on a post?
What place for haunting
Would you like the most?
      Now, what would you do?

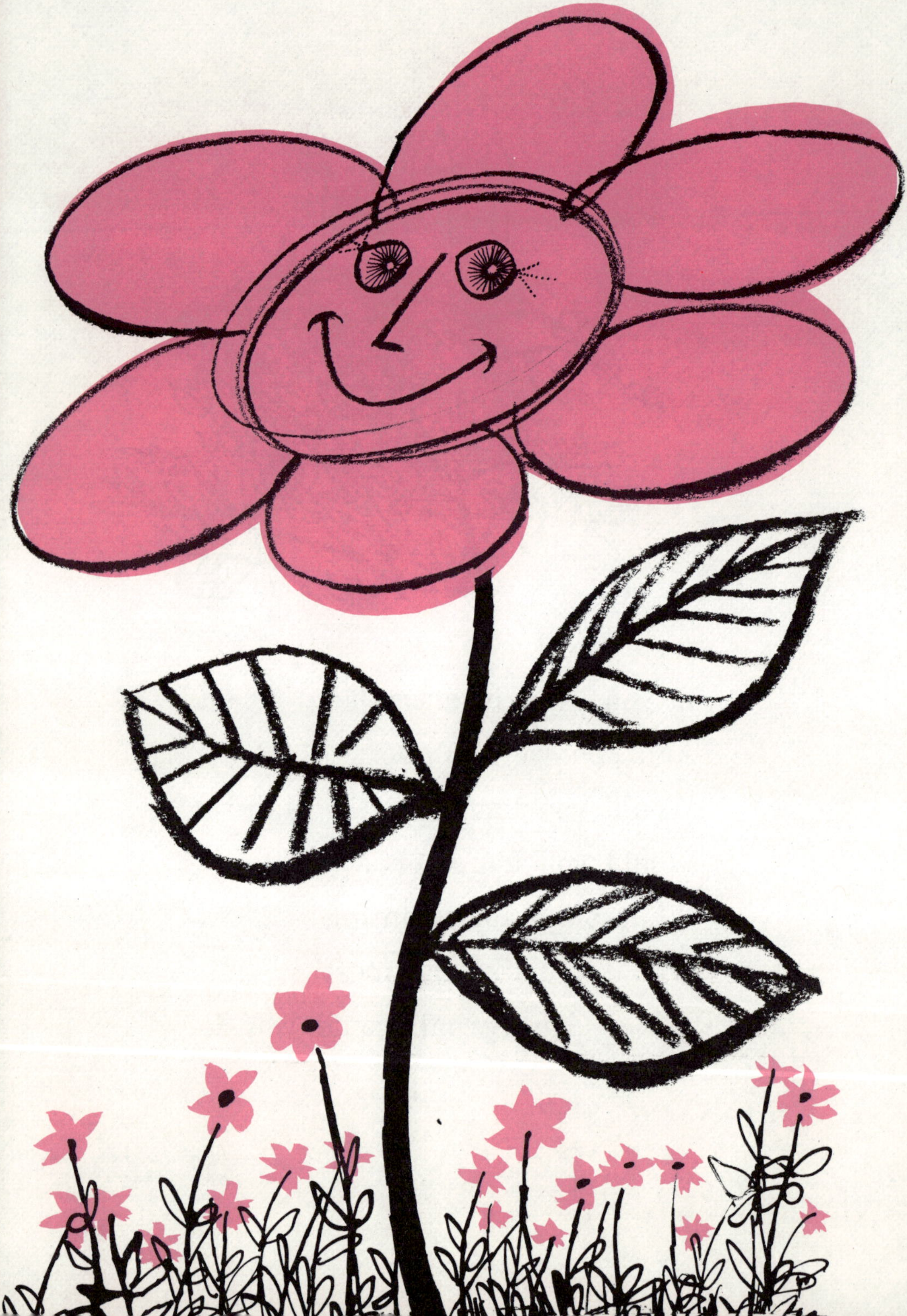

If you were a pixie,
After a shower
Would you
Dry the face
Of every wet flower?
If you were one
Of the pixie men,
Would you help
The flowers
Smile again?
      Would you?

If you were an elf
And the moon shone bright,
If you were an elf
In the moon's clear light,
    Would you sing,
    Would you dance
With all your might
Through all the hours of the night?
    What would you do?

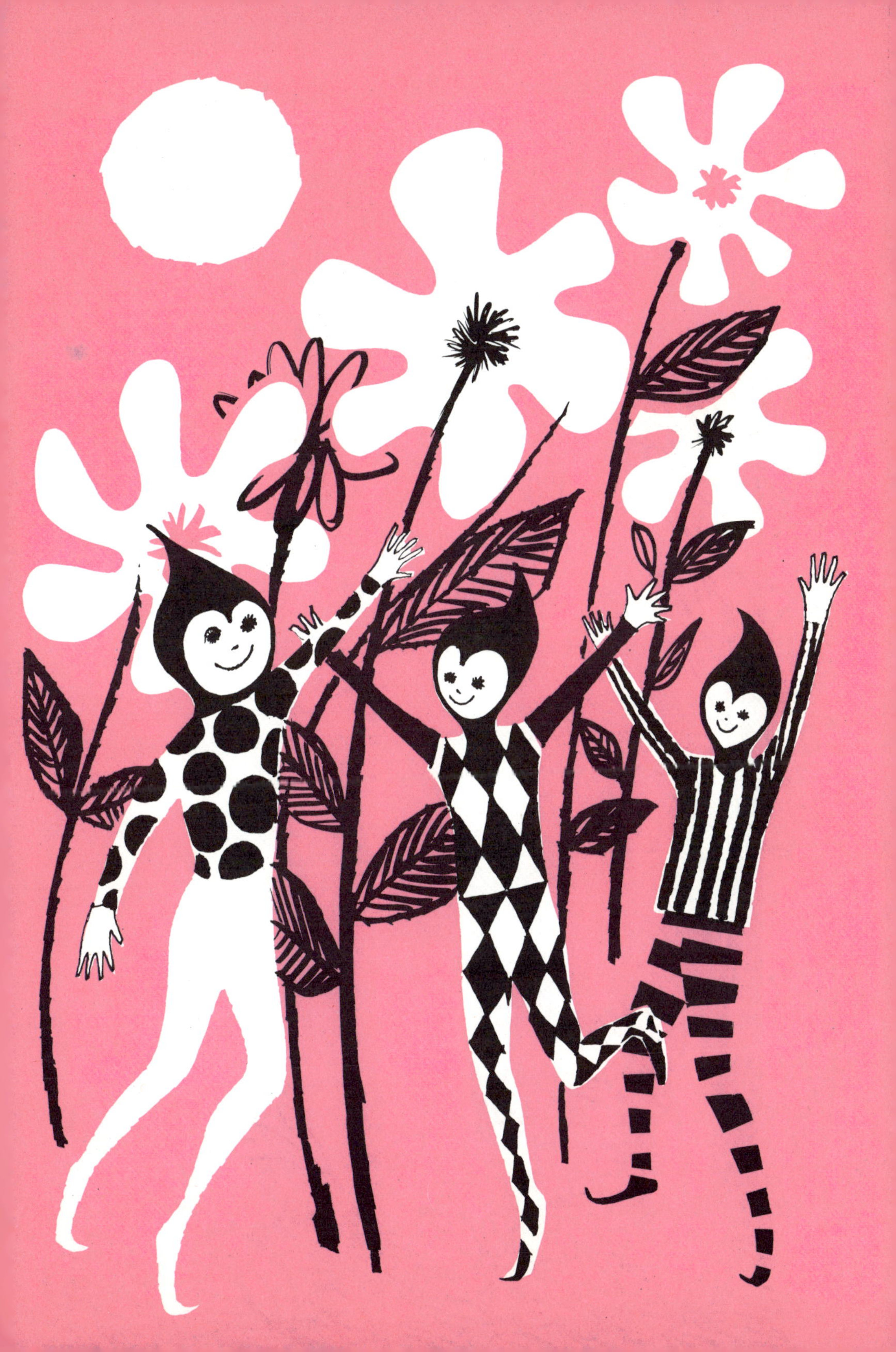

If you were Jack Frost
In the clear, cold air,
Would you push down the leaves
Till the trees were bare,
And send the leaves flying
    Everywhere?
        Would you do that?

If the wind
Took your kite
Way up high
For a sail,
With you hanging tight
To your kite's
Long tail,
        Then what would you do?

What would you do
If your rabbit came in
With a coat to cover
His furry skin?
Would you smile to see him
Standing there?
Or might you borrow
His coat to wear?
      Well, what would you do?

57

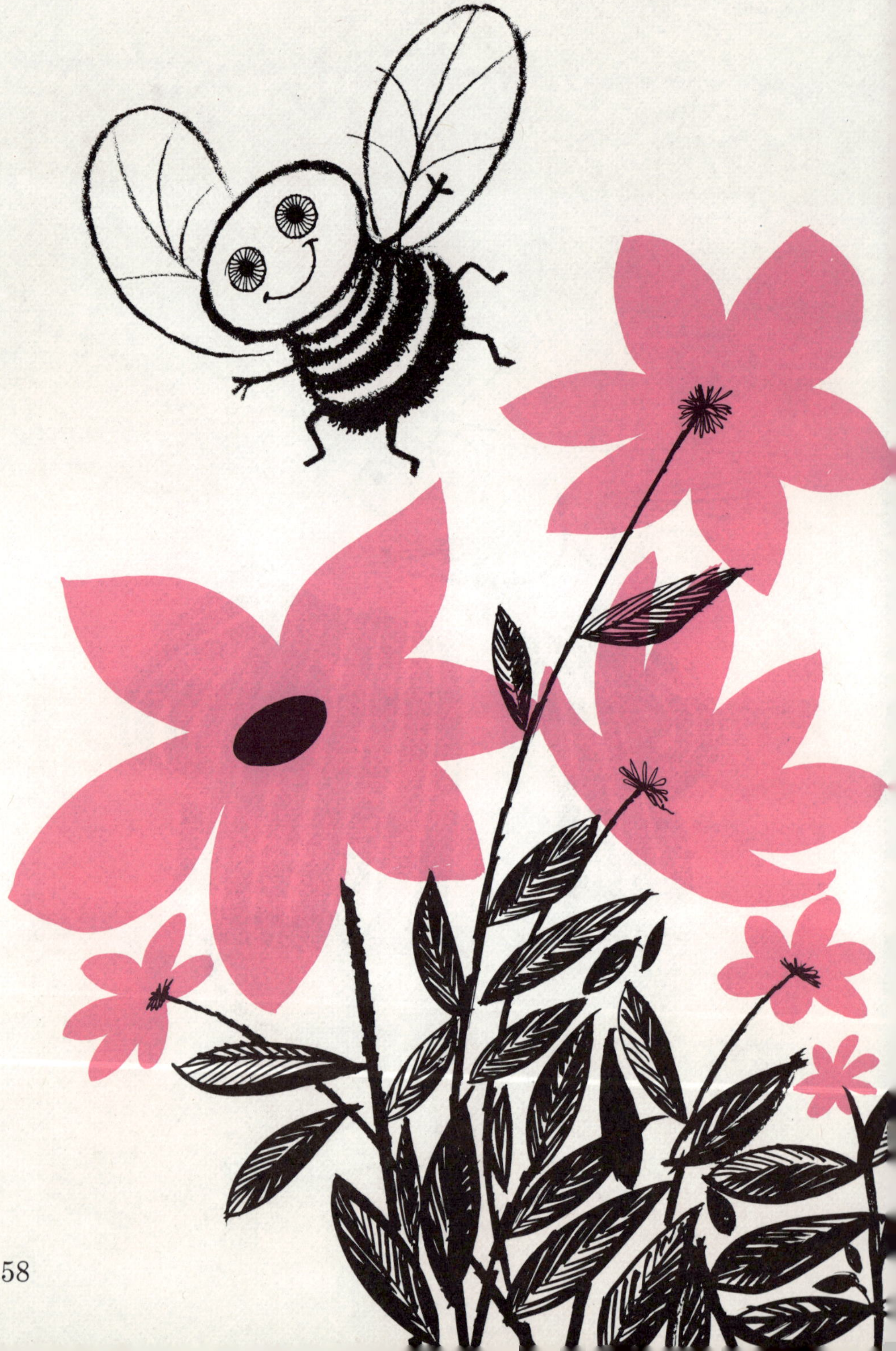

If you saw a bee,
And he saw you,
And he came
Buzzing
Right toward you,
Do you know
What you would do?
      What would you do?

If you had a dog
Who liked to play
By wagging his tail
And running away,
What would you
Think of him?
What would you say?
      What would you do?

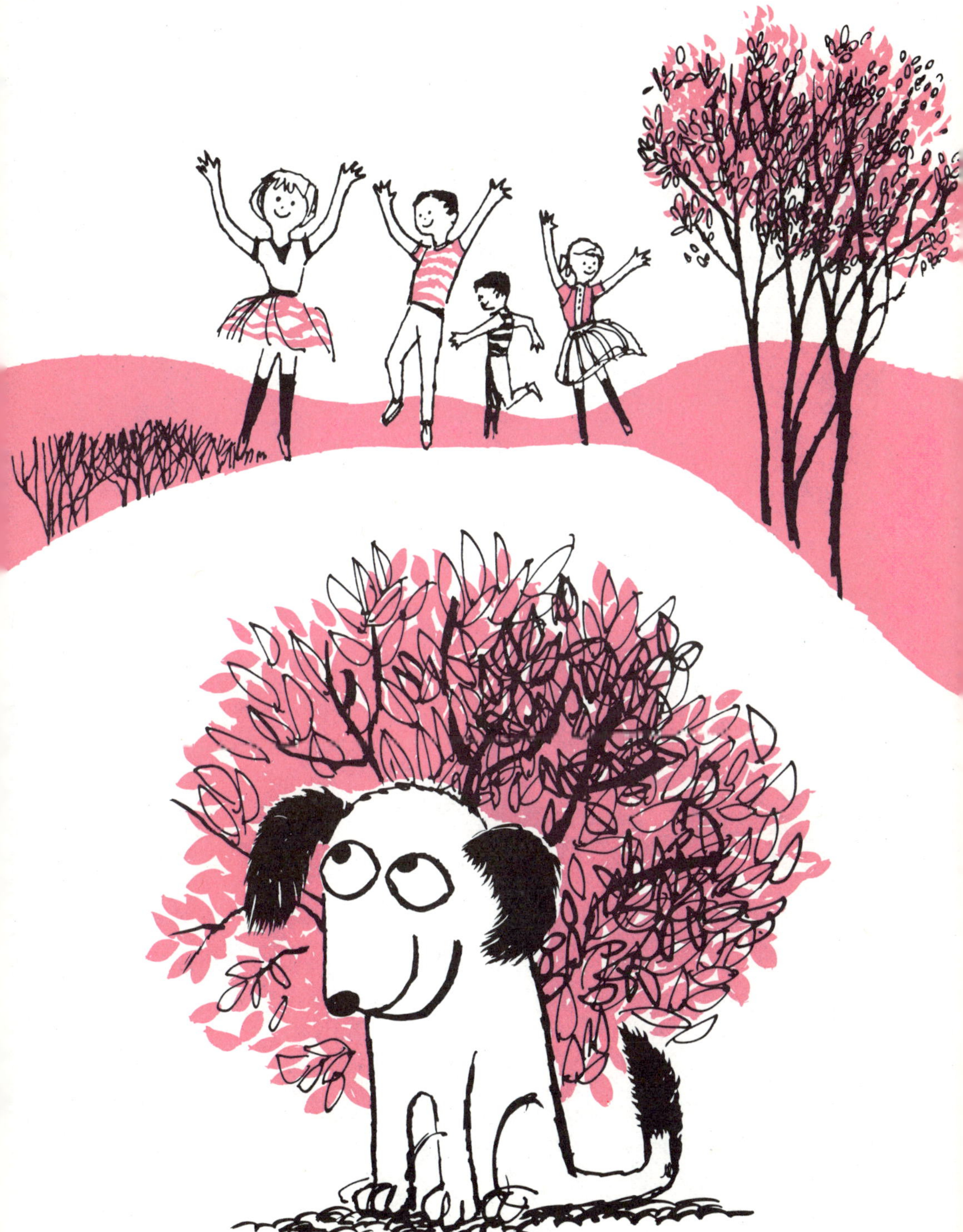

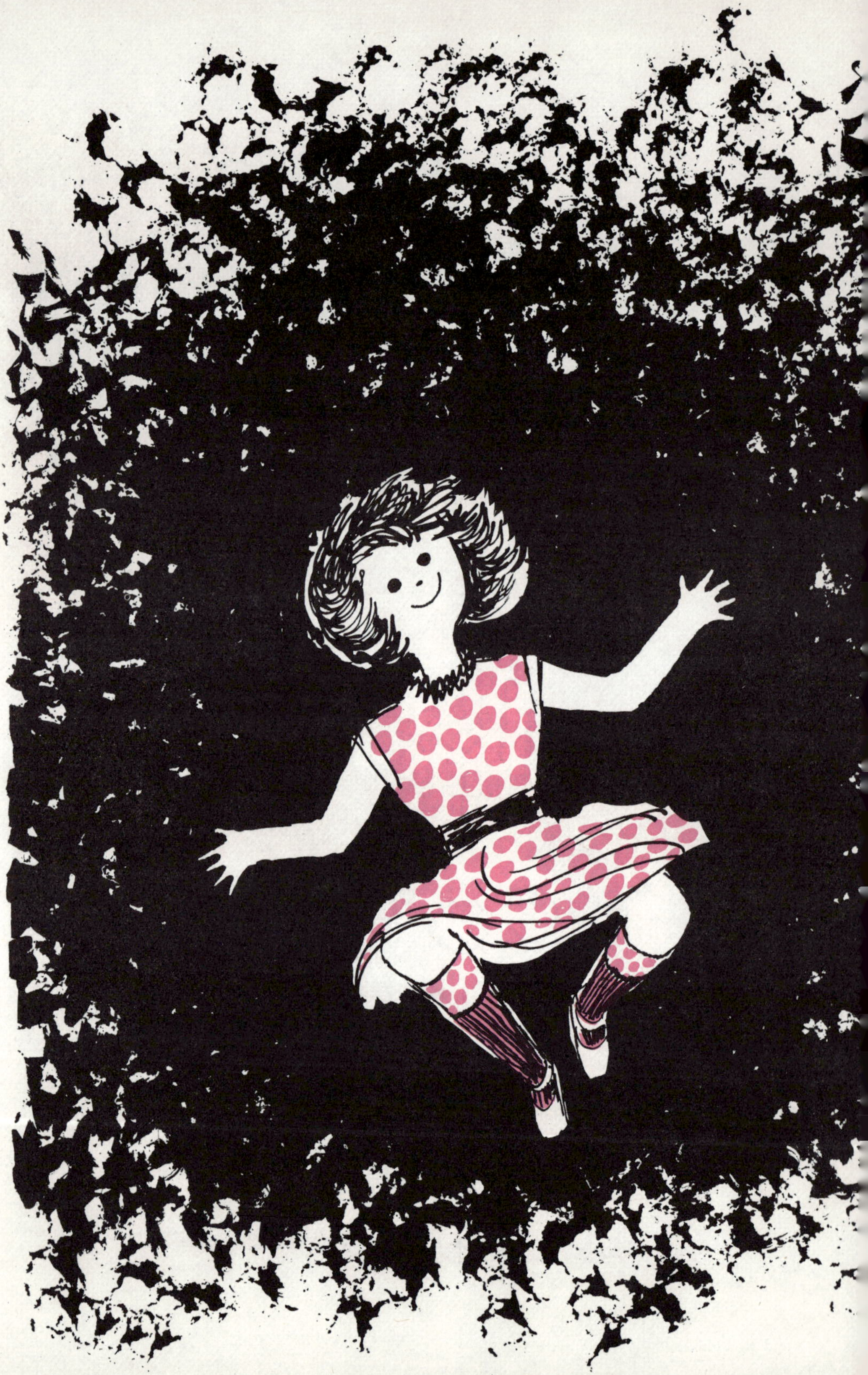

What would you do
If you jumped so high
You found yourself
Going way up in the sky
And might not get back
Till the first of July?
Would you laugh?
Would you cry?
          Oh, what would you do?

If you told a story,
Which one might you tell?
A story of monsters?
Or an old witch's spell?
Or of horses, of rabbits?
Or of gold in a well?
      Or what would you tell?
      What would you tell?